CW00926162

Praise for Donna Ashworth

'Donna Ashworth has a way of formulating words that melts me … I feel as if the universe has sent me her book to tell me I'm on the right course.'
Davina McCall

'Powerful and comforting … Donna's words could change your life.'
Dawn French

'Absolutely beautiful … Whenever I'm feeling lost, I reach for Donna Ashworth's words and feel found.'
Bryony Gordon

'Some people have the Bible by their bed. Others a self-help manual. I have Donna Ashworth.'
Susannah Constantine

'If there is a god, Donna is doing her or his work.'
Robbie Williams

'So inspiring, so heartfelt … the way Donna writes is beyond beautiful.'
Lisa Snowdon

'Soul-nurturing permission to relax, connect and be kinder to ourselves.'
Fearne Cotton

'A little corner of calm within life's storm – wonderful.'
Cat Deeley

'Donna's words are never just words, they are teachings. Provoking and inspiring, comforting and loving, I couldn't live without them.'
Kellie Bright

'Donna's much-needed words will no doubt empower and lift our young people today.'
Lisa Faulkner

'Like a warm hug. Donna's words are comfort for the soul.'
Tamzin Outhwaite

'Donna is a true wordsmith. Her writings never fail to move me.'
Nadia Sawalha

'Donna has a rare gift of being able to put into words how we all feel. Her writing is like a hug from a wise friend.'
Samia Longchambon

To the Women

Also by Donna Ashworth:

The Right Words

I Wish I Knew

Life

Love

Loss

Wild Hope

Growing Brave

Words to Live By: A Daily Journal

DONNA ASHWORTH

To the Women

Black&White

First published by Donna Ashworth in 2020
This updated and expanded edition first published in the UK
in 2024 by Black & White Publishing
An imprint of Bonnier Books UK
5th Floor, HYLO, 103–105 Bunhill Row, London, EC1Y 8LZ
Owned by Bonnier Books Sveavägen 56, Stockholm, Sweden

Hardback ISBN: 978-1-7853-0716-4
eBook ISBN: 978-1-7853-0809-3
Audio ISBN: 978-1-7853-0824-6

A CIP catalogue record for this book is available from the British Library.

Typeset by Envy Design Ltd
Printed and bound in Great Britain by Clays Ltd, Elcograf S.p.A

3 5 7 9 10 8 6 4 2

Every reasonable effort has been made to trace copyright-holders
of material reproduced in this book. If any have been inadvertently
overlooked, the publisher would be glad to hear from them.

Black & White Publishing is an imprint of Bonnier Books UK
www.bonnierbooks.co.uk

To Emma, Lauren and Becs.

I hear you still.

66

What incredible creatures we are
born of star, as soft as the ocean that
carves out the land with creation and
birth in the palm of our hands

99

AUTHOR'S NOTE

Thank you for picking up this book. I think of that act like opening the jewellery box we treasured as children. The light switches on, the music sparks into a comforting song and the dancer begins to turn … magic is afoot. I would love to tell you a little bit about this book and what she may bring to you.

I self-published the original version of this book in 2020, the year the world locked down, and I had no idea at the time how it would change my life.

The poems within came from a period of me seeking female connection, a sisterhood. I was floundering in my world. Unsure of what I was doing, where I was going and what I wanted out of my time here on this earth. Becoming a mother had slowed me down in a way and allowed me to readjust my perspective enough to see that the rat race was no longer serving. I was tired. Tired of running too fast all the time and yet never seeming to be able to keep up.

I knew, instinctively, that without one another we women are not as centred and strong as we could be. We need to come together, we were always supposed to come together, for it's in the sharing of the secrets that the solutions lie. And this thread that bonds us stretches back through time and much adversity.

I figured I would stand above the introverted parapet and wave a hand to see who came. And many, many of you came. Soon, we were sharing and encouraging one another daily. Standing at the back of strangers online and finding solace in the knowledge that whatever you are facing, you are never alone.

Someone else has faced it too, and the telling of their story can be the saving of yours.

The book came out, I nervously awaited your thoughts and struggled with my own demons as I did so. I had boxed myself in with fear by this stage of my life. I had believed the word on the street that women above forty, *mums*, can't do anything exciting or new. But my inner child was constantly singing to me otherwise. I let her out. And I never looked back.

You bought the book, you gifted the book, you gave one to every friend you had and passed it out at yoga groups, retreats, schools and more. It was a whirlwind of connection, far greater than I had hoped for, and it hasn't stopped since. My little inner voice was right. We truly need one another. The strength of the right words, at the right time, is limitless, and this book gave you all a thread to stitch into your lives in the most beautiful of ways – a thing that is credited entirely to you and your kindness, intuition and grace. I simply put down the pages and let her fly.

So here we are. Four years later. I have added much to this book because I have lived much and learned much, but, for the most part, I kept the bones of her intact. After all, it's important that we accept and honour the versions of ourselves we have been in the past.

The bottom line, my friends, is that women know. From generations of knowing and long lines of women who knew, we all grew. And we grow still. To ensure the women *we* raise are paved a better path. For that is our responsibility, this I truly believe. We shout so that those behind us can hear.

We scream so that those who are silenced can be heard. We share so that someone is saved. And we do it every day.

what incredible creatures we are, born of star
as soft as the ocean that carves out the land
with creation and birth in the palm of our hands

I hope you see yourself in here. I hope you *see* yourself full stop. In all your glory. And I hope it reminds you what you have come through and who you are. A random page a day, for the message you need … the book knows, just like we do.

CONTENTS

Roots deep
leaves tilted towards the
light and on we grow

DESERVING

We women know
that freedom lives in the *choices*
and that our choices from day to day
can often be consumed
with our need to support others
to support *everyone*

it is common to place ourselves last

and yet, we women
look at other women
and immediately see their *deserving*

we immediately identify the absolute need
for self-care and moments of calm
no question of worthiness or earning

perhaps, if we will not allocate ourselves this grace
we could pretend to be seeing another?

step outside yourself today and *see*
with eyes free of self-sabotage

what is it that you need?

BE THAT WOMAN

Be the kind of woman you want to call
when things go wrong
be the motivator, the encourager of dreams
be the kind of fierce friend you want to have yourself

love your girlfriends deeply
they are your sister warriors in this world
and only they know just what a crazy, hormonal ride
womanhood really is

be loyal, love hard, be a soulmate
be a sister, be strong, be kind
listen hard and laugh lots
tell the truth but keep the secrets

big up every woman you meet
kind words travel endlessly
if you can't say anything nice
look more closely

spread the sparkle of a smile
and a compliment whenever you can
there is room for us all to be happy and successful
lend a hand if you're there already
pull your girls up, push them if you need to

straighten each other's crowns
spot the lipstick on the teeth
and the loo paper on the shoes
avoid the drama, smile at the haters
they're actually admiring you from afar.

IT'S TIME

There comes a day, somewhere in every woman's life
when she is hand-delivered a message from Mother
Nature herself, with vital words scrawled lovingly but
emphatically upon it ...

It's time

you have taken enough now
it's time to stop growing up, stop growing older
and start growing wilder and wiser

there are adventures still waiting on you and this time
you will enjoy them with the vision of wisdom
and the companionship of hindsight
and you will really let go

it's time to stop the madness of comparison
the ridicule of schedule and conformity
and start experiencing the joys that a life
free of containment and guilt can bring

she will remind you gently
that you've done your bit
you've given too much, cared too much
you've suffered too much

you've bought the book, as it were
and worn the T-shirt

worse, you've worn the chains
and carried the weight of a burden
far too heavy for your shoulders

it's time, she will say

let it go, really let it go and feel the freedom
of the fresh, clean spaces within you
fill them with discovery, love and laughter

fill yourself so full you will no longer fear what is ahead
and instead you will greet each day
with the excitement of a child once more

she will remind you
that if you choose to stop caring
what other people think of you
and begin caring what **you** think of you
you will experience a new era of your life
you never dreamed possible

it's time, she will say ...

to write the ending, or new beginning
of your own story.

JUST BEGIN

There is a fine line between trusting the process and waiting for something to happen. And the word to focus on here is *waiting*. Don't wait. Just begin. There is always one teeny tiny step you can take towards your dream, whilst the universe is busy engineering your next bridge. And if you are not in the action of *doing*, as well as *being*, within your mental wishing well – then waiting is wasting your precious time. Begin. You don't need to be ready. The word *ready* has prevented more dreams being realised than anything else because we can never be fully ready. It is important that we begin imperfectly. And afraid. And carry on just like that too. The magic only truly sparks when wonky wheels are in motion. Don't wait. Just begin. The process starts with you standing up and saying, *let's go* …

TO THE WOMAN WHO THINKS SHE ISN'T GOOD ENOUGH

To the woman who looks around and wonders
why everyone else is so much more capable
so much stronger
so much more ambitious than her

to the woman who thinks everyone else
is blazing a fiery path through this thing we call life
whilst she limps behind
barely getting through the days

somewhere, another woman is looking at you
thinking exactly the same

you see, we all look like we're nailing it
from the outside in

we all look *together* sometimes
catch us on the right day and hey
we look like we have it all
because guess what
we learned to look that way a long time ago
we learned to hide our struggles behind a smile
and whack on that mask every day

and actually, we are doing each other a favour
when we show up just as we are
warts and all, late, flustered
human

what we really need to see
is that we are all the same
we all struggle, we all fall apart

some days we nail it, other days we get nailed
by hiding our own weaknesses, fears, worries
we give them more power
if you let it out, shine a light on it all
it becomes so much less scary, funny even ...
and goodness only knows we need to laugh

so, to the woman who wonders
if she is good enough ...

if this is you
yes, you are
you always were

you don't have to live up
to everyone's expectation
of how you should be coping

you are human, flawed, wonderful
miraculous, loveable, loved

I see you

now do me a favour and go see all the others too

spread the word, we are good enough
just as we are.

"

I scaled further away
from my life and its worry
until perspective shifted
and cropped out the hurry

"

PERSPECTIVE

I climbed the biggest hill I could find
each step evacuating
my overcluttered mind

breath falling into rhythm
lungs billowed full-sized
like sails at high mast
to ride with the tide

and with each step
and with each breath

I scaled further away
from my life and its worry
until perspective shifted
and cropped out the hurry

until this life looked very small
and I could *see*

the only thing that needs
to be moved, is me

everything I truly need
grows amidst the leafy trees
and ebbs and flows

in carefree breeze.

A SUCCESSFUL WOMAN

I know a successful woman. She has mastered the
art of this being human. She works hard but when
she is home, she cares more about whether her plants
have grown. And sends out love to her hatchlings
who've flown. She has time to think, to sleep and
to play. She loves travel but is content on an ordinary
day. She makes money, just enough, to fund all of the
above. She is *living*. When she is at work, she works,
and when she is with friends, she is there. And when
she is gardening, or talking, or cooking, she radiates
such *care*. She has built a world with enough room
to grow. And everything is used, not a thing is there
for *show*. I think success might mean: more time and
space. And the gratitude to host life with grace.
I know a successful woman. She has mastered the art
of this being human. She is giving by letting things
go. And I want to be her when I grow.

WHEN THINGS CALM DOWN

You vow to reconvene
when things calm down
when life slows a little
when you get through this next phase

but the truth is
life does what you instruct it to
and it will only truly calm down
if you command it

the calm must begin with you
and radiate out in waves
washing over each part of your world

an ocean in full flow
whispering slow slow slow

the only rush here, my friends
is in the things you have marked
for later

you have them the wrong way around

this life is what you allow
make it now now now.

BOUNCE-BACK

Dear Life-Bringers, Dear Creators, Dear Mamas

Do not, for a moment, tolerate this notion of bounce-back, after childbirth. Your body took nine months to stretch, evolve and re-form, so that it may make a whole new life. It will absolutely take that, or more, to return. And if it does not come back to exactly how it was, it is really little wonder. You made a PERSON. Your body did its best, but if it feels lacking, look at what it gave you. Look at what it gave you, my love, and be in awe of all you are. You are life, you are woman, you are a humanity-maker. Bounce-back is for balls, and you don't have those. What you do have is a doorway to creation.

What a thing indeed.

"

I am not bereft
the love has not left, this nest
it simply rests

"

A RESTING NEST

My nest is not empty
it is resting
it is still full, of love
the legacy of lives which grew, and flew
every giggle, every tear
was nurtured here

and I am not empty
I am resting
I am still full, of love
and the unending possibility of more
walking back, hand in hand
through that very front door
I am not bereft
the love has not left, this nest
it simply rests

till it's time to nurture calls
till noise and laughter grace the walls
once more

the heart keeps the score
I am watching love soar.

WOMEN CAN HAVE IT ALL

I think women can have it all
as long as the all, is including the small
and not this dream blindly handed down
by circus clowns, on a merry-go-round

we can have love, lots of that
pure friendships, messy homes
with imperfect parts, the mess is *art*
and we must have messy lives
for happy hearts

we can have space, to weed out shame
disapproval and disgrace

we can have peace
but peace comes only with the final release
of perfection, and no clear direction

we can have success
if failure is an ingredient not an impediment
this life is no experiment
it is universally, spell-bindingly sent

we can have it all, every drop
and it starts with seeing
what we've got.

DON'T THINK

If you are a writer, an artist, a musician, a creator
of any kind (or you'd like to be) … don't think too
much. That's my advice. There is a space, you see …
between thoughts, feelings and existence, which is
where the magic happens. And you can only get there
by shutting off your computer brain. Switching gears,
as it were, into your soul brain (it's a thing). The
real, true gifts are made without planning, without
spreadsheets, without practical thought of any kind
whatsoever, until much later. If you want to create,
I think you shouldn't think. Just do.

Shine your brave
light brightly
so your people
will find you

DEAR FRIEND

I'm sorry for being so bloody rubbish
but you see, life moves really, *really* fast
from the minute I open my eyes
there are people relying on me
for many different reasons
some of them involve eating and basic survival

I am spinning plates and dropping plenty
you, my dear friend, are one of those plates
but I love you very much
I wish that every text message I wrote to you in my head
made it into the virtual space and into your phone
to let you know you're in my heart and on my mind
I wish I could carry through with all the plans we make
knowing we never will
I go there in my mind – it's loads of fun

when I drop, frazzled, into bed at night
I remember I haven't rung you, again
then I remember I haven't locked the back door
or brought the cat in and just like that
it's happened again and I have forgotten, again

I am very hopeful that one day life will be easier
and we will be blessed with plenty of time
stick with me, I promise I will be worth it
when we are old and grey
and you need someone to laugh with, I'm there

Yours loyally
Your bloody rubbish friend.

A COLD DRINK ON A HOT DAY

There will always be someone in this life
who just doesn't like you
no matter how hard you try to please them

there will always be something you say or do
which causes offence or division
whether you mean to or not
there will always be someone who finds fault in you
your life or your words
you may never find out why
please don't waste your precious time trying to

you cannot be everyone's cup of tea

then there will be those who like you on impact
a little fizz of energy that passes between you
silently, unseen, bonding

those people will not only like you
but they will like you wildly
they are your people
whatever precious spare time you have
pray spend it on them

you can't be everyone's cup of tea
but you can be someone's first sip of a cold drink on a
hot day
or a warming hot chocolate coming in from the cold
or the pop of a long-awaited champagne cork
or a stiff shot of tequila when things go awry

find your people, love them hard.

ELASTICITY

I know we shouldn't judge a woman's appearance,
but oh how I get excited when I see an unapologetic
wrinkle or a swathe of silver hair worn fiercely in
its splendour. I can't help it. If you are smooth and
youthful and that makes you feel strong in midlife,
then I am happy for you, my friend. But if you are
leading the way into the wilderness of wisdom-hood,
like a queen choosing bareness for battle, no longer
reliant on tight skin for tight self-worth, then I am
grateful for your light. And I follow it. Seeing you go
forth gives me strength to accept this truth of living:
we are *supposed* to lose our elasticity outside,
and absorb it all within.

THEY'RE WATCHING

They're watching, you know
when you get to the beach
and you linger self-conscious
the sea out of reach

they're listening each time
you deny yourself treats
in order to punish
the fails of last week

they're watching, you know
when you stare at your shape
disgust in your eyes
your face full of hate

they're listening to you
when you say *no I can't*
when you put yourself down
when you rage and you rant

they're watching, you know
so give them a show
a guide for a lifetime
of letting things go

a manual for love
a map for the stars
a self-regulation
to heal any scar

show them perfection
is not on your list
that life is chaotic
but beauty persists

allow them to see you
make friends with yourself
and show them acceptance
above anything else

they're watching, you know
those sweet little eyes
so show them a life
not lived in disguise.

EVERY WOMAN KNOWS

Every woman knows pain. It is silently lived with
for so long. Every woman knows change. It is faced,
fear and all, from so very young. Every woman knows
the juggle. Spinning plates and catching balls like a
circus in full swing. Every woman knows worry, for
the world we were given, the world we created and the
world we wish we could save. Every woman knows
nights unslept with a mind too full. And every woman
knows, how pain and joy walk so closely in step. Every
woman knows, that every woman knows: coming
together, judgement-free and heart wide open, *helps*.
Hearts wide open today, my friends. We can't do this
without each other.

HAPPY NEW YEAR

When I say *happy new year*
I'm not for a moment
expecting this to occur
for that is not possible

a year must be *all things*

happiness must come and go
like the tides and the winds
just as sadness
and all the emotions in between

when I say *happy new year*
I'm really wishing you
a baseline of peace
of gratitude
of courage

because if you can sit
with these things
for the most part

happiness will thrive
when it does arrive

and sadness will know
its place in the mix

if you can nourish these things
daily
you will also grow hope
for it flourishes in such soil

and hope is the key
to this enigmatic state
of *happiness* we seek

when I say *happy new year*
I'm really wishing you
more happy days
than sad days
more joy than misery
more laughter than tears
more bravery than fear

and the wisdom to accept
that they all belong

happy new year, my friends

happy new year.

FIND A GOOD LIGHT

If I'm looking to take a nice photo, I always search for a good light. Whether I'm outside or in, there is always a beam coming from somewhere … and if you stand in it and smile from your soul, you will glow. Matters not what you look like. And this thought is a great analogy for life. Especially as the darker months roll in. *Find a good light to stand in.* There are so many ways to do this, figuratively and literally. And on days when light is scarce, the habit of seeking it out, practically and mentally, is one that will stock your woodpile high. And you need your woodpile well stocked, my friends. You must protect that beautiful light of yours, because you may not even realise it, but it leads the way for many.

TO OUR DAUGHTERS

You were born made of softness
sweetness and love
but with a will so strong it could bend iron
despite what society may tell you
you don't have to lose one or the other
keep them all, they are yours

your superpower in this life
is that little voice inside that tells you
when something isn't right, listen to it
likewise, listen to it when it's saying *yes, yes, yes*

your self-worth is controlled by you, *only you*
never put it in someone else's hands

you are equal to, not better than, but equal to
anyone else you may ever come across in this life
never feel inferior

never lose your joy
no matter how serious your ambition
or how driven your path
remember we are here for only a short time
and life is to be lived and loved

comparison will not propel you ahead
rather it will keep you back
from the real treasures in this world
stop comparing
better still, never start

fear is an instinct, but unlike your inner voice
it can be misleading
never let fear hold you back
from the wonders you could see

do not let society tell you
what beauty looks like
if you feel beautiful, you are
if you see beauty, it's there
your beauty is an amalgamation of everything
that makes you *you*
and it is utterly unique
embrace that, fully

we women have the ability
to be all things to all people
but remember yourself
put yourself first too

lastly, it is okay not to be okay
it is even better if you talk about it
darkness cannot shine through light
but light can shine through darkness

you can be amazing and admired
whilst admitting your weaknesses
and discussing your fears and anxieties
even more so, in fact

oh, and never let anyone dull your sparkle
you were born to shine.

THE ANGRY IMPOSTER

I don't know who needs to hear this, but your imposter syndrome is supposed to be furious. She literally exists to hold you back and keep you small, so her anger, therefore, is the litmus test to your bravery. If it is rising, so is your authenticity. If her blood is boiling, chances are you are cooking up something creative and courageous. If she is quiet and calm, something in your flow may need to be released. Your imposter syndrome is supposed to be spitting and fitting, with incredulity, at your audacity to shine despite daily chains of negativity wrapped around your light. Keep making her mad. That's the sign you're in the right lane.

ONE DAY

One day an army of furious older women
might just take over this world
and I want to be there, at the front

because one day
every woman wakes up and realises
that quite frankly
they put themselves through hell
trying to fit in
trying to be enough
to be attractive, to be acceptable
to be responsible, to be reliable
to be a mother, to be a wife
to be a friend, a carer
to hold a career
to keep it all spinning effortlessly

and in a flash, years and years
of back-breaking conformity
whizzes before your eyes
and you have a lightbulb moment

it was never going to happen
we could never have done it all
for it is not possible
no man could do it either
not a chance

women of this world
beautiful, wonderful women
let that lightbulb go on sooner
rather than later
because when it does
you will be free

free to live
free to mess up
free to take breaks
and make mistakes
free to pass over on the list of things
you *should* be doing
to understand that
whatever you did today
was enough

you are enough

one day
an army of furious older women
might just take over the world
and I want to be right there

at the front.

THE GREYS, THE WRINKLES

The greys, the wrinkles, the rolls, the dimples
don't strip you of your grace
the lines, the weight, the clothes that pinch
don't steal light from your face

if you could see what I can see
your world would open wide
the way your smile lights up the sky
the soul you have inside

the greys, the wrinkles, the rolls, the dimples
don't wash you of your wonder
the lines, the weight, the clothes that pinch
aren't worthy of your anger

if you could see what I see now
such beauty carved through time
you'd grieve the years you missed that joy
the tears and wasted time

the greys, the wrinkles, the rolls, the dimples
don't steal away your light
but the way you talk down to yourself
those harmful thoughts, just might.

When you
embrace your flaws
someone watching
finds their way

MISS ME MOST

When you feel you are without me, close your eyes.
Float down beneath your skin, retreat within. I am
the blood that flows, I am the courage in your gut that
grows. I am the chamber in your heart that feels like
home. I am the seed from which your life was proudly
grown. Only my body has flown. But me, I dwell still
within your bones. My voice and all the good I've
ever known, is yours to own. When you feel you are
without me, listen close. I whisper louder, when you
miss me most.

MIDDLE FINGER

By 40, our middle finger is at half-mast
By 50, it's full on UP
By 60, both of those fingers are hoisted in a V
and not a single care is given anymore

I mean, we care about our family
our friends and our passions
we care about the environment
we care about equality and living in peace
but we don't care about *fitting in*
and we don't care
what people think of us
not anymore

too many years were wasted on that

we certainly don't care to stay quiet
or bite our tongues
we haven't wasted all these lessons
to play dumb
when the situation calls for our wisdom

neither do we care if our waistline
is the acceptable size
or if our thighs are toned and unblemished

we have wrinkles, stretch marks
war wounds, warts and all
and we are rocking each and every one of them
in all their glory

you see, there comes a time
in every woman's life
when you realise that this is it
this is the time to be alive

to live without restriction or oppression
to break free of the chains
society binds us with and tear loose

this is our time to be
completely and totally
who we were supposed to be
all along
the sooner you get there
the better

life waits for no woman.

MOMENTS THAT MAKE LIFE BETTER

Summer sunsets and dawn illuminations. A baby's giggle. A nap in the sun. The sound of the ocean. A hot bath after cold rain. Fresh sheets on weary bones. Taking off your shoes. And your bra. Running fast then laughing hard. Dancing like a lunatic. Licking the spoon. Finally getting to lay down your tired head. Realising how grateful you are to be safe. Cosy chairs on frosty days. A shared joke. A message from a friend right on time. A cool breeze in the baking heat. Morning cuddles with time to spare. Sunshine through clouds. The breaking sound of birdsong after a long winter. Hearing *I love you*. Finally letting it go. Making friends with yourself. Realising that magic is everywhere. If you look.

"

You took your deepest suffering
and mixed it with forgiveness

"

ALCHEMIST

You took your weeping wounds
and stitched them into safe spaces
gardens in which love could grow

you took your deepest suffering
and mixed it with forgiveness
until its colour bloomed
with gold and orange
like the first sunrise of a fresh start

you took your past
yanked on its chain
pulled it out at the root
and wrapped it around your breaking bones
until it softened like butter
spreading out its submission
for those coming next

you are not just woman, just mother
just wife, just lover
you are an alchemist

a maker of magic from dirt.

DON'T LET THEM MAKE YOU UGLY

No matter how someone stamps all over your heart, your loyalty, your kind nature, never let them make you ugly. For beauty comes from within, and nothing turns skin more sour than bitterness, hate and regret. Let them throw whatever they want at you, if they must, then step away. Learn a lesson. Don't go back for more – your time is far too precious for that. Instead, use your time to heal, to process the pain, to move on. A little stronger, somewhat more guarded, but never bitter. Your beauty will shine on and attract like-minded souls into your orbit. And the more you refuse the hate and the toxicity, the less those people will come into your life. You are a mirror that they cannot bear to look into, you see. A beautiful soul. Don't let them make you ugly, my friend. The world is ugly enough.

THERE WILL BE DAYS

There will be days, my friend
when you feel like you can't go on
just keep swimming
breathe in, breathe out and wait
for the light of a new day to dawn

there will be days, my friend
when nothing seems to be making sense
it's not supposed to
clear your mind and open your heart
the answers will come in time

there will be days, my friend
when the pain rises up to engulf you
be kind to yourself
lay low and let the tears flow like a river
release, open the floodgates, let it out

there will be days, my friend
when it feels like
the whole world is against you
when it feels like you cannot do right
for doing wrong
just sit it out

tomorrow is a new day
and these feelings will pass
I promise

you see, life is all things
from one day to the next

it is beautiful at times
wondrous, amazing and joyful
then it is awful
miserable and heartbreaking

and the cycle goes around
it is as it should be
everything is as it should be
and you, you will be okay

have faith
keep hope in your heart
tomorrow is a new day.

"

Mum, you have given me the
very best start, you made a home
within your heart

"

MUM

If I could ribbon-tie the moon and the stars, the oceans and the earth, it would not make a gift worthy of your love. Mum, you have given me the very best start, you made a home within your heart. You showed me what love is. And how to give. Without tearing parts of myself in the process. How to never feel less than enough. You gave me grace to embrace the smooth and courage to face the rough. When life gets tough, it is you I channel, your voice I hear. Your advice and your wisdom I carry ever near. And always will. No matter where you are, I will listen to you still. Thank you, Mum, for all I have become.

AGE GRACEFULLY

Age gracefully, they say
but I fear that what they mean
is age quietly, slip aside
be wise but stay unseen

age gracefully, they say
but I think, they're afraid
that we may all wear purple
and wrap silver hair in braids

age gracefully, they say
don't succumb to the knife
but don't let standards drop
don't wear your clothes too tight

age gracefully, they say
but don't be looking old
likewise, not too young
take your place, fit the mould

age gracefully, they say
but grace means, being at ease
flowing with the winds of change
so, doing as we please

age gracefully, age tastefully
age like a fine red wine
just age with your acceptance
and you'll never fear the lines

age gracefully, my friends
whatever path you tread
walk it with your own permission
it's your home, so make your bed.

"

I like you enough to wish
I was better

"

SORRY

Sorry
about my roots ... the state of me
my chipped nails ... the mess of my kitchen
I don't have much in the fridge ... I can't come
I didn't text back ... I'm not great company
for the tears again ... it's only a little something

all these things we apologise for
could be eradicated and replaced
with one simple statement

I like you enough to wish I was better

and if we said that, straight out
the reply would be

I like you enough not to give a toss.

TEN THINGS TIME HAS TAUGHT ME

Most of our life is spent
chasing false goals
and worshipping fake ideals
the day you realise this
is the day you really start to live

you really, truly cannot please
all of the people all of the time
please yourself
and your loved ones first
everyone else is busy doing the same

fighting the ageing process
is like trying to catch the wind
go with it
your body is changing
but it always has been
don't waste time trying to reverse that
instead change your mindset
to see the beauty in the new

nobody is perfect
and nobody is truly happy with their lot
when that sinks in you are free
of comparison and free of judgement
it's liberating

no one really sees what you do right
everyone sees what you do wrong
when that becomes clear to you
you will start doing things for the right reasons
and you will be far more fulfilled
and have much more fun

you will regret the years
you spent berating your looks
the sooner you can make peace
with the vessel your soul lives in, the better

your body is amazing and important
but it does not define you

your health is obviously important
but stress, fear and worry
are far more damaging
than any delicious food you may deny yourself
acceptance and peace are the best medicines

who will remember you and for what
become important factors as you age
your love and your wisdom will live on far longer
than any material thing you can pass down
tell your stories
they can travel farther than
you can imagine

we are not here for long
but if you are living against the wind
it can feel like a life sentence
life should not feel like a chore
it should feel like an adventure

always, always, use the things
you keep for 'best'
tomorrow is guaranteed to no one
today is a gift
that's why we call it the present

be peaceful, be loved
and be merry.

"

Fighting the ageing process
is like trying to catch the wind

"

HOLD TIGHT

In those moments, when darkness is unbroken by light,
hold tight. To your core. To the belief that there is more.
That light will return, and soon. It will crack through the
curtains and fill this very room. Stay afloat, by holding
yourself like a safety rope. Until someone else can hold
you too, the safest place in this world, must be you. Hear
the truth. Not the voices who tell you you're useless and
used. You're just bruised. And bruises heal. Hunker
down and feel. This is simply passing through. In the
way all feelings do. Hold tight, to you.

66

If I could strew your way with flowers
bring you sunshine every hour
I would, I would

99

IF I COULD WRAP YOU UP

If I could clear your path of stones
break the sticks to save your bones
I would, I would

if I could strew your way with flowers
bring you sunshine every hour
I would, I would

if I could shield your heart from pain
give you strength to rise again
I would, I would

if I could take those from your life
who tear you down and bring you strife
I would, I would

my child, it hurts to let you go
in a world so full of hate and woe
and though I know it must be done
you'll always be my little one

if I could wrap you up again
I would, I would.

BORN WITHOUT A WORRY

You were born not caring much
about the curves along your thighs
and it took you several years
to care a thing about your size

when you die, I'm kind of thinking
that your thoughts won't stray to that
you won't waste your final breath
to utter words of being too fat

yet the years spent in between
from your birth till you depart
when your life is there for living
when you're young, alive and smart

are the years you waste with worry
for the way your nose sticks out
or the changes in your body
you can't do anything about

and those years may seem aplenty
but for some they end too soon
what if you had not embraced them
whilst your world was in full bloom

so, remember how you frolicked
little child of untamed glory
it's not too late to change your thoughts
not too late, to change your story.

ALL THE ANSWERS IN NATURE

The sky doesn't feel shame
for letting loose a hurricane
it just calmly carries on
releasing sunshine and birdsong
… *what's gone is simply gone*

the ocean will not falter
throw itself upon the altar
for waves that crossed their lines
the ocean knows it was her time
… *to crash hard and realign*

the trees that bare it all
drop their leaves and let them fall
because Mother Nature called
know the answer to it all
… *is to let go and never stall*

and you with all your faces
all that life in all those places
starting new and leaving traces
of human heart and soul
knowing acceptance is the goal

you were supposed to be it *all*.

❝

You are a work of art
a work of learning
a walking story

❞

BLANK CANVAS

You started with a blank canvas
beautiful, unspoiled, that much is true
then life began to mould you, shape you
draw its art upon your skin
stretch marks, freckles, sun spots
wrinkles, laughter lines and frown lines
and every time something new
appeared upon you
you mourned the loss of the smooth
unspoiled and innocent
what you failed to recognise is that
the beauty of your journey
the true strength of your fight
is now etched upon you forevermore
you are a work of art
a work of learning
a walking story
a beautiful, broken warrior
it was always meant to be so
if you must change something
change the way you see it, my friend
change the way you see it
there is much beauty you are missing.

Let it go
you need that space
for something
far more wonderful

REMEMBER HER

Somewhere inside of you
there's a little firecracker
with her arms folded and a frown on her face
she isn't happy, you forgot
to set her a place, at your table
that you are no longer willing nor able
to frolic in the sea, reckless and free

she is sad about all the times you said yes
accepted second best
when you should have said no
when you should have let it go

she is mad about all the times you said no
when you could have given over to the flow
of this life, it's not to be lived in strife

she wanted you to buy the ticket
she wanted you to take that trip
she definitely wanted you to take that risk
that may have just opened a whole new world
she is quite smart, this little girl

she wants you to remember
the wonder in glowing embers of a campfire

the joy of lying still
under a sky coloured sapphire

to face the day without fear in your heart
and embrace every opportunity that comes
take every opportunity to *run*

she doesn't understand why
you won't wear the swimsuit
she doesn't understand why
you won't eat the cake
she doesn't understand why
you continue to fake

somewhere inside of you
there is a little girl
who wonders at the adult you've become
she did not sign up to a life lived
out of the sun

she still has many things she wants to learn
and so many people still to meet
she still has food she'd like to taste
and parties for her dancing feet

she still has places she wants to go to
and wonders she can't wait to show you

somewhere inside of you, all of you
there is a little firecracker
desperate to see more

of this thing we call life

go get her, she is fun.

SPLASH

Your kids will remember you getting in the water with them. Any water. They'll remember how they splashed you hard and you laughed this time and splashed them back. They will honestly remember, we all do, the feeling that summer was just the time of our lives, when problems solved themselves and people came together in different and oh so special ways. It matters not what you pay for or where you go, it matters only *how* you go. So, if you are not in the water, metaphorically and literally, for reasons within your control, I hope you run, jump and dive-bomb like a five-year-old high on sugar. Because this is the stuff that sticks, my friend. These memories live in the simple moments, that only summer can provide. Make a splash.

"

I will bring what you need with pleasure
and I will listen to your problems
without measure

"

I DON'T NEED YOU AT YOUR BEST

I don't need you at your best
when you come to my home
I don't care what you are wearing
or what car you drove here
I don't care if there is food on your shirt
and your hair is full of knots
none of that matters to me
I care about you
I care about what's in your heart
how afraid you are
what you worry about in the night
I care about your deepest fears
and your biggest dreams
and I am there for it all
if you mess up, I won't judge
that's my promise to you
so don't cancel my visit
because your house is a mess
and your cupboards are bare
I will bring what you need with pleasure
and I will listen to your problems
without measure
if you are on the floor, I'm picking you up
or I'm sitting down beside you
you need never be alone down there
and before I leave, I will have made you smile
at least once
that's my promise to you
so, save your best for someone else, my friend
because I want you, just as you are
that's what friends are for.

DUCKS IN A ROW

I do hope your ducks aren't in a row. I pray your eggs
aren't all in the same basket and I definitely don't
wish your ship to be tightly run. Life happens in the
space between perfect and free, you see. And joy
cannot slip through cracks if there are none, nor can
love grow wildly in a garden that's paved without a
weed in sight. Growth needs a mix of battering rain
and pure, unfiltered sunlight. Messy is holy. And
free is the prize. Breathe out that stifled sigh and lie,
hand on your beating chest. You came here to rise
and rest, amidst the eggs in many baskets. And ducks
waddling as they please. Cares all flowing wildly, as
they must, into the breeze.

TO THE WOMAN WHO IS SLOWLY FADING AWAY

To the woman who has lost her spark
to the woman whose get up and go
has well and truly gone
this is for you

this is to remind you
that you don't have to be everything
to everyone, every day
you didn't sign up for that

remember when you used to laugh, sing
throw caution to the wind?
remember when you used to forgive yourself
more quickly
for not always being perfect?

you can get that back again
you really can

and that doesn't have to mean
letting people down
or walking away
it just means being kinder to you
feeling brave enough
to say no sometimes
being brave enough
to stop sometimes and rest

it starts the moment you realise
that you're not quite who
you used to be
some of that is good
some of that is not

there are parts of you
which need to be brought back
and if anyone in your life
is not okay with that
they are not your people

your people will be glad
to see that spark flicker back

so, if you have been
slowly fading away, my friend
this is the time to start saying yes
to things that bring you joy
and no to things that don't

it's really pretty simple.

AGEING

Ageing isn't about lost youth, it's about finding. Who
your true friends really are. The difference between
shiny and worthy. The confidence to be yourself in any
room. The time to dedicate to the things that bring
you joy. The wisdom to say no to the things that don't.
The freedom to choose your own path in life. The
courage to be happy in your own skin. The knowledge
that very little really truly matters, in the end. Ageing
isn't about lost youth, my friends, no, it is not. I haven't
lost a thing, in fact. Except, perhaps, my ability to
give a toss about the things that won't matter when
I'm gone. No, ageing isn't about lost youth, it's about
finding. Finding who you were meant to be,
all along.

ARE YOU GOOD?

When you were but just two weeks old
they asked me, are you good?
and waited, as I scoured my soul
for ways to not sound rude

you do not sleep more than an hour
or feed the way you should
but look at this sweet little face
to count the ways you're good

you're made of half my partner
and the other half is me
and yet I see my granny
and two mighty family trees

you've lived within my body
for the past nine months or so
and now you're there and breathing
is there more they need to know?

I longed for you for years
and worried day and night
I prayed you would be healthy
and here you are, just right

so yes, you're good, my baby
you are as good as good can get
and this is just the start
there's so much more *good* to come yet

and whilst I seem half-human
as I nurture your small bones
my colours will return
I won't remember cries and moans

so yes, my love, you are very good
if this is what they mean
each day you cry is a day alive
and every mother's dream.

PUMPKIN SPICE

The people who get excited about pumpkin spice
are teaching us how to be content. They sense the
warmth fading, summer sighing its last, but you
won't hear their lament. They won't wail or repent
the longer days and shorter nights. No, they simply
go forth and create their *own* light. They seek
shining nuggets of joy, like a child finally holding
that coveted toy. In bookstores and coffee shops, they
fill their hearths with autumn's lot. Cold noses raised
aloft, to *see*, what their soul truly needs. Pumpkin
spice and all things nice. That's what these people
are made of.

A PHOTO OF A WOMAN

There was a photo of a woman
on the internet
she was smiling as she splashed
amidst the sea
I read the comments underneath
and this is what they said
her body is just way too big for me

there was a photo of a woman
on the internet
she was laughing and dancing
life seemed good
I read the comments underneath
and this is what they said
she's way too skinny
give that girl some food

there was a photo of a woman
on the internet
she was asking everyone
to buy some shakes
I read the comments underneath
and this is what they said
I won't buy from you
if you can't lose your weight

there was a photo of a young girl
on the internet
a mother's post
to say that she had passed
I read the comments underneath
and this is what they said
why did she suffer
why did she not ask?

I see so many photos
on the internet
and so many have so little good to say
and I was thinking, maybe
it's our words
which need to change
maybe, we could find
a kinder way?

YOU'RE SOMEBODY'S HERO

Today, remember that the bad times
are part of your journey too
they are part of your story
so own them, never let them own you
these challenges that you face
you are supposed to be facing them
you are supposed to come out victorious too
this is just another chapter in your book

never underestimate the power
of your hardships
they will inspire others
they will create waves that ripple on for years
they will help others to face their own demons
and come out fighting

you see, it's not just the good chapters
of our stories
that people will want to read about
we all need a hero to look up to
right now, everything you're going through
makes you somebody's hero
so, put on your cape and get it done, girl
then shout it out from the rooftops
that you survived
your story could be someone's saving.

GUT FEELINGS

Gut feelings are like guardian angels
listen very closely to those little messages
that start in your tummy and try very hard to be heard
they may be the voices of those who walk with you
your guardian angels doing their thing

pay attention to the hairs
that bristle on the back of your neck
for when that happens
you have been touched from above
by someone who has your very best interests at heart

what is it they heard that made them connect?
go back, find it
listen

if you are struggling to make a decision, my friend
say it out loud
as though you were talking to a loved one
and wait for the feelings that follow

you are never, ever alone
you are always being guided in everything that you do
likewise, when your instincts are screaming at you to leave
to free yourself, to move on to better things
listen hard, they are right

pay close attention to the voices deep inside
they are your guardian angels

listen.

Perfection is a myth
we must stop
believing in

WHEN YOUR HEAD HITS THE PILLOW

Remember the smiles of the day
the laughter, the warm words
and let everything else go
put the lessons learned
in a file marked *done*
and give yourself a pat on the back
for the things you got right

leave the stresses of tomorrow
where they belong, tomorrow
leave the stresses of today
where they belong too
and let the night take away
the heavy weight
from your shoulders

let it go, let yourself be safe
let yourself be still
let yourself be at rest

when your head hits the pillow tonight
let sleep come
and let your soul regenerate
for a new day

you did your best today
you did enough
we are all just doing our best
with no rule book
in a game with no referee
and no half-time
none of us are getting it right
we are all just winging it

we are all just as scared
just as weary

when your head hits the pillow tonight
close your eyes

and remember you are worthy

choose peace.

WAVE THE WHITE FLAG

There are many choices available
to us women in this life
but when it comes to your body
there are only two
accept it, or don't

you see, if you choose to accept your body
you will soon start to love it
admire it, look after it

these things all follow
in the wake of your acceptance

when you realise
that this vessel for your soul
for your spirit
is an instrument of such high design
and fine-tuning
that it boggles the mind
to even think about

you will enter into a phase
which I like to call
peace, at last

you will care nothing
of spare fat, grey hairs, loose skin

you will realise, eventually
that the body's purpose is not to look good
to attract friends, partners, successes

that it is, in fact, your spirit
which does all of those things
if you would only allow it
to shine through and work its magic

your body, my friends
has but one job
to see you safely through
this adventure of life
to allow your spirit
to reach its potential
that is it

if you are on the path
of not accepting your body
you are in for a very long battle
against an enemy
you have no power to defeat
nature, time, biology, fate
you don't have the weapons
to fight those powers

wave the white flag
give in, accept
it is then
that your life will truly begin.

"

You are not walking alone
this floor you crashed on
has become your throne

"

WARRIOR

You didn't ask to become a warrior
nonetheless, here you are
half human, half scar
you are healing, by feeling
by allowing yourself to go *there*
to the times life left you naked and bare

and you hold that girl, so scared
let her know, there is a long way to go
but you are not walking alone
this floor you crashed on
has become your throne
and using all you have ever known
you have grown
into a version of she
the world had no idea
you could ever be

you did not ask to become a warrior
but a warrior you have become
a soldier of the sun
and your weapon of choice

is to forgive everyone.

THERE WAS A TIME

There was a time
I would have set myself on fire
to keep others warm

there was a time
I would have crossed oceans
to reach people
who wouldn't cross a stream for me

there was a time
I would try, too hard
to be seen by those
who would simply never see me

there was a time
I felt myself unworthy of a person
who could actually
never be worthy of me
but not anymore

you see, my friend
there are many ways
to spend your time on this earth
but wasting it on those
who are not appreciative
of your attention
is a crying shame

use your time wisely

save your best efforts
for those who care
for those who would return the favour
or at least appreciate your attention
those who truly value you

and the rest?
if they do not see you now
they likely never will
and they are missing out

make this the time when you realise
your time is precious
and should only be bestowed upon those
who bring you comfort, positivity
support, love or joy
or all of the above

remember, you are the main act
not a warm-up
and this, my friend
is no dress rehearsal
this is it
the curtain is well and truly up
shine on.

MIDLIFE MUSE

If you are struggling to find your way in midlife and beyond, find yourself a muse. They are out there. Shining silver goddesses, stylish and fierce. Open books with wisdom and knowing spilling out of every page. They will remind you, these visions of growth, that you are here to change. That you can choose who you will become next, that leaving behind a version of you is not just normal, it is absolutely vital. They will lead you to your new you, the one that cares not for comparison or expectation. The one that is determinedly taking up space and breaking through concrete with fresh shoots of life. Do not ever stop reaching, my friend. There will be women one day soon who will need to see the brave footsteps you made.

TO BE A WOMAN

What's it like to be a woman?
a little bird whispered in my ear
is it just like being human?
oh, it is so much more, my dear

we are the holders, we are the keepers
of the secrets and the truth
we are the safe place in a storm
the creator of all youth

we are the place where life is softest
we are the colour in the story
we are the wisdom and the instinct
Mother Nature in all her glory

we are the taker of all worry
we keep it deep within our hearts
so that others may unburden
so that great new lives may start

we are the makers of the home
not just the walls but of the spirit
bringing everyone together
letting love and laughter fill it

we are sisters, mothers, wives
so many things in every day
we are the start of every life
we are the reason, we are the way

we are fuelled by intuition
call it magic, if you like
we are women, so much more
than any words that I could write.

"

You are truly treasured
if my love was to be measured
it would take forever

"

SON

What an honour it has been to see you grow. To be the
comfort, the safe place, to which you always go. I have
long held your growing hand, and will do the very same,
as I did, from boy to man. I hope you always understand,
my heart is never closed to yours. Sweet boy, you have
shown me the beauty in laughter, the joy of watching
your happy-ever-after, is my dream. But in those times in
between, remember your roots. Pull up your socks and
strap your boots, for you are truly treasured. If my love
was to be measured. It would take forever. And more.
My mothering heart is an endless open door. And you,
my son, are the wings on which it soars.

WOMAN, MIGHTY, PROUD

As a girl I often noted
that my gender stood me well
I felt powered by a *knowing*
like a magic in my cells

propelled by intuition
I could sense deceit and fear
I would hear true words intended
though they never crossed my ear

and then somebody told me
that girls were second best
they said we must work harder
play the game and sit the test

and this just made no sense
to my young enquiring mind
how dare they call me less
when I'm a warrior, womankind

I flow with healing power
like the women gone before
centuries of creation
banished cruelly to the floor

and now the world is waking
to the ideas we knew then
that gender does not rank us
or decide who prospers when

ceilings crash in sparkling shards
with which we fashion thrones
connected by the female threads
that grow within our bones

refuse to rest in deference
chin up, girls, raise your heads
come dance in moonlit woodland
the patriarchy's dead

as a girl I often noted
that my gender did me proud
and to this day I take my space
woman, mighty, loud.

WHEN YOU SAY GOODBYE TO A PARENT

You are suddenly living in a whole new world

you are no longer *the child*
and regardless of how long
you have officially been *grown up* for
you realise you actually never were
until this moment
the shock of this adjustment
will shake your very core

when you have finally said goodbye
to both your parents
assuming you were lucky enough to have had two
you are an orphan on this earth
and that never, ever gets easier to take
no matter how old and grey you are yourself
and no matter how many children
of your own you may have

you see, a part of your body
is physically connected
to the people who created it
and also a part of your soul
even if the thread is not blood but choice

when they no longer live
it is as if you are missing something practical
like a finger or an arm
because really, you are
you are missing your parent

and that is something
far more necessary than any limb

and yet the connection is so strong
it carries on somehow
no one knows how exactly
but they are there
in some way, shape or form
they are still guiding you
if you listen closely enough
you can hear the words they would choose

you can feel the warmth of their approval
their smile when a goal is achieved
their all-consuming love filling the air around you
when a baby is born

if you watch your children very closely
you will see that they too have a connection
they will say things that resonate with you
because it brings so many memories
of the parent you are missing
they will carry on traits, thoughts and sometimes
they will even see them in their dreams

this is not something we can explain

love is a very mystical and wondrous entity

it is far better to have loved and lost
than never to have loved at all
and grief, grief is the price of that love
the deeper the love, the stronger the grief

when you say goodbye to a parent
do not forget to connect with that little girl
who still lives inside you somewhere
take very good care of her
for she will be alone and scared

when you say goodbye to your parents
you lose an identity, a place in the world
when the people who put you on this earth
are no longer here, it changes everything
look after yourself the way they looked after you.

66

You can feel the warmth of their approval
their smile when a goal is achieved
their all-consuming love filling the air

99

YOU'RE GOING TO LOSE PEOPLE

You are going to lose people along the way. People you thought you'd never lose. People you truly believed would always be there. And it's going to hurt like hell. But that is life. People change, relationships change, some evolve, some disintegrate, some people leave through no will of their own, and that hurts the most. They didn't want to go. But you, you will survive it all. You will look back and realise that the people you need, really need, are still here, in some way, and that the other relationships you lost along the way have taught you something that made you better. And that's life. Hold close those who are in your life now and regret nothing. Use the feelings of pain to commit to a life here and now, a life where you take no one or nothing for granted, where you cherish every minute with those people you love. You're going to lose people along the way, but that is life, every minute counts.

WOMAN IN MY MIRROR

There's a woman in my mirror
and she looks a lot like me
though there's lines around her eyes
and her hair is wild and free

she is plumper than myself
and she is definitely grey
did I miss the day this happened
has she always been this way?

and this woman in the mirror
has an air of something calm
like a tide that's going out
and a beach that's soft and warm

she has seen the world in colour
she has learned to know the truth
there's a wisdom in her wrinkles
there's a knowledge brought from youth

and she seems to move more freely
as though released from earthly binds
is she made of something lighter?
perhaps the weight she left behind

like the press of expectation
and the need to yield and bend
I like this woman in the mirror
she's fast becoming my best friend.

Look how far
you have come
you are a warrior and
you are not done yet

IF YOU WOKE UP TODAY

If you woke up today
with a mountain in your way
and your energy
has all got up and gone

if your heart is set to break
and the stress you just can't take
let the world around you
march and carry on

don't be scared to take a seat
and to admit a short defeat
it's not wrong to lose the will
once in a while

let your body shed its weight
give your mind a tiny break
let your thoughts flow free
breathe deeply, find your smile

you only get one time alive
and it's vital that you thrive
you're a living breathing human
full of wonder

you need water, you need sun
you need food and you need fun
to take time out to charge
or you'll go under

it's not you who's full of fault
it's the world which needs to halt
don't confuse your weary heart
with something broken

we all keep a too fast pace
this is life, it's not a race
listen hard, my friend
and hear the truths I've spoken.

"

You can't reach for anything
new if your hands are full of
yesterday's trash

"

SET IT DOWN

You must feel so heavy with the weight of all that expectation ... set it down. The guilt, the worry, the fear, the comparison, the expectation of others. It's too heavy. Set it down. You can't reach for anything new if your hands are full of yesterday's trash. And your heart needs space to cultivate all that is light and all that is your right. So, set it down, my friend. Leave it there, walk away. It was never yours to carry anyway.

THE ART OF AGEING GRACEFULLY

Think about it

you have earned this face
every line, a laugh shared
every wrinkle, a year survived
every age spot, a day that
the sun shone on you

some women believe that as they age
they lose their looks
oh, my friends, how wrong this is
a beautiful young woman
is a happy accident of nature
but a beautiful older woman?
she is a work of art

the Japanese have a practice whereby
they repair any broken objects with gold
believing that something which is broken
has earned its beauty
and should be celebrated
and decorated
rather than discarded

I feel this way about women
it took a long time to find out
who you really, truly are
a long time
the acceptance that old age brings is freeing
it brings with it peace and happiness
everyone knows
happiness looks good on us all

allow your face to represent your life
your stories, your joys
ride with it, accept it, embrace it
be amazed by it

why choose to be an older woman
fervently chasing youth
when you could be that older woman
who knows what she is worth
and has earned every minute
of her hard-won self-acceptance

the trick with ageing successfully, my friend
is to pay as little attention to it as possible.

"

Be there for the dark moments and
then enjoy the light together.

"

THAT'S FRIENDSHIP

Be there for the messy parts of someone's life,
don't be afraid of the ugly. Hold someone's hand
when no one else can, or will. Pull them to stand.
Be there for the dark moments and then enjoy the
light together. Don't take a seat at a celebratory
table if you won't be there to collect the shattered
pieces when that same world falls apart. It's easy to
get an invite to someone's pretty, someone's sparkly,
but if you get invited to someone's raw and real,
show up, you have been blessed. That's friendship.

TO YOU WHO WILL LOVE MY SON

It is hard, so hard, to imagine a day
when I will not be the moon
the sun and the sky
to my little man

when he is sad
he calls for me
when he is scared
it's me he wants
when he feels excited
I am the one he rushes to tell first

I am the keeper of his secrets
the finder of anything which is lost
and the solver of any known problem
in his little world
I am his everything and he is mine

one day, you will have the pleasure
of being his everything
one day, it will be you that he comes to
and that is, of course, the way it should be

but I hope
you will think of me sometimes
perhaps let me be amongst the first
to hear some good news
or allow me the honour
of pulling you both
out of some trouble
life may throw at you

I will be waiting, ready and willing
I will not meddle or fuss
or pull you in opposite directions
I promise you that

and should you be blessed
with children of your own
there will be no one
no one on this earth other than you
who will love them more than I

the bond between a mother and a son
is divine, this much is true

but I wish for him
the very same bond with you
and I pray the circle of love
goes on and on and on
much further than me

after all, that is what
I brought him up to do

love.

"

The very same hormones that
see you freely cry are the reason the
entire human race is still alive

"

SERIOUS TEARS

These hormones, which plague us so and see us weeping at the drop of an emotional hat, are life itself. This one race of ours would not be here today without the soft hearts and nurture of women rearing babies, children (and one another) in a hard and nasty world. We are the reason. We are the women who bring up the next generation. Over and over again. Always with love at the heart. These hormones keep us vulnerable, it is true, but for very good reason. We are here to love, nothing else, and those hormones bring us back into that place of beauty and creation. These *silly* tears we shed are actually quite serious indeed. Dead serious, in fact. *The very same hormones that see you freely cry are the reason the entire human race is still alive.*

DEAR WOMEN

Maybe you don't know
just how amazing you are
maybe you don't see
how you keep everyone going
even when you're struggling yourself
maybe you don't realise
how much cheer you bring others
regardless of your own level of happiness
maybe you don't see the smiles you spread
or the joy you bring
maybe you don't know what an amazing effect
you have on the world you created
well, you should know
you are the kind of women we all need
when things get hard
you hang on, when the wind blows
and even better than that
you keep others hanging on too
you, my friend, are a wonderful creation
how do I know this?
because your ability to inspire
and support other women
brought you here somehow
you are wonderful
you should really see that
I do.

A BACKSTAGE TOUR

Getting older is like being given a backstage tour.
Without the lights, the sets, the music, suddenly you see
the whole production for what it is: a show. You catch
a glimpse of the star without makeup, getting ready to
go home. And you realise she is not the superhuman
entity you thought her to be. She is just a person, like
you; they all are, we all are. Getting older is like being
given a manual on life, decades too late or, perhaps, right
on time. Suddenly it all makes sense and you no longer
focus or pay attention to the wrong things, the false
idols. Getting older is being given the gift of time. Even
though time is running out, you value it so much more,
that every minute is worth a hundred. Getting older is a
privilege denied to many, grab it with both hands
and breathe it in.

FRESH NEW START

They say you choose your body
when your soul is free of hate
you see it for its wonder
and the joy it will create

and then throughout your childhood
you pay no heed nor care
to the way your flesh is growing
or the wave within your hair

it starts when neuro-pathways
in your brain begin to form
based on how you're loved
and the examples you are shown

and so those little pathways
are joined to pathways new
the ones that carry feelings
from your heart to be reviewed

and if those neurons fuse
with the wrong emotion-spark
it's safe to say your life
will ever play out in the dark

so take your time to grow
the pathways of your mind
and don't think it's too late
there is time to break that bind

just hold your shoulders tight
in a hug straight from your heart
meet your eyes right in the mirror
and make a fresh new start.

UNDERNEATH IT ALL

It's never as good as it looks ... other people's lives.
Perspective and distance create a glossy lens to view
through. The truth is, no one is exempt from pain.
From the agony of loss. The daily toxicity of unhealed
bonds. From friends who ghost or colleagues who
berate. From the hurt of watching our children learn
hard truths, or the fatigue of fast fading elderly family.
We all know the universal downs. No matter the highs
and their smiling shared snapshots. And your
own life ... it's never as bad as it looks, either. When
you are inside it, weighed down and unable to see the
view clearly. In times of unbearable pressure, go to
the middle ground and *see*. Despite a few daily details,
everyone is pretty much (bare bones on the table)
exactly the same. Underneath it all.

TILL THE SUN RISES AGAIN

There will be
some very painful moments
in your life, my friend

there will be moments, days even
when the sun doesn't seem to rise in your sky
and the breath feels sucked right out of your lungs

when food has no taste, the world has no joy
and everything seems like an effort too far

yes, my friend
there will be
some very painful moments in your life
but you will get through them
this too shall pass

because life has a way of throwing you a rope
just at the very moment when you thought
you couldn't swim another stroke
all you have to do is grab it

and one day, as is the way of this life
the sun will suddenly beat down
on your face again
and the air will feel fresher
than it ever did
and there will be laughter
and love
and joy
so much joy

and life will be sweet again
like summer after a long winter
a winter that was so dark
each colour that appears
feels like the first time you are seeing it

this is when you must live, really live

for, just as the bad times
do not last forever
neither do the good
this too shall pass

so, embrace the joy when it comes
and let fear slide away
and when the dark times
come around again
and they will, remember
you have what you need to survive
and you will survive, my friend
you really will

keep the important people close
focus on what truly matters
and you will find yourself dragged to safety
each and every time the storms come

and on those days
when the sun is high in your sky
but you notice another
facing bad weather
you drop your raft
and you go to them
and if they won't climb in
with you, to safety
you simply stay with them
in the stormy water
till the sun rises again
and it will

it always does.

"

For, just as the bad times
do not last forever
neither do the good
this too shall pass

"

FIND MY WORTH

Don't define me by my size
you won't find my worth in there
see no measure in my thighs
or the colour of my hair

don't judge me on possessions
or the holidays I take
don't wonder of my treasures
or the money I may make

I'm a mixture of emotion
all rolled into a form
full of life and love and laughter
and memories so warm

I'm all the lands I've wandered
and the stories that I've read
I'm all the thoughts that visit
when I rest at last in bed

I'm a complex mix of lessons
which I've learned along the way
I'm an echo of my musings
and the things I didn't say

I'm often fiercely happy
and sometimes deeply sad
I'm kind and deep and loving
for that I'm truly glad

so, look at me and wonder
at all that's deep inside
don't just assume you know me
and the stories my smile hides

if you take the time to delve
you will find out more each day
but, for now, no need to judge me
till you've walked with me some way.

Tomorrow the sun
will rise again
and so, my friend
will you

A LANTERN FOR YOUR SOUL

I made a little lantern
the day your lungs drew breath
I sparked a bright eternal flame
and set it in our nest

I let that little lantern shine
on every move you made
it washed our worlds with nurture
it grew you, where you laid

and as you grew, I grew with you
and the lantern kept alight
it warmed our days and often saved
our souls in deepest night

and when you flew, deep down I knew
the lantern must go too
to light your way through storm and rage
its glow emboldening you

I didn't need this light, you see
all mothers know this truth
my soul is fed each time you tread
the path your heart's drawn to

so keep our little lantern safe
and never dim its shine
your worth is fuel, your heart a jewel
know this and you'll be fine

the light I made, the love I gave
will burn forevermore
and when you cannot see that fire
dig deep a little more.

HEAVEN

Follow me, she said
I'm going somewhere new
it's not a place on any map
it's deep inside of you
you can't get there by car
or boat or any train
you get there just by feeling
by switching off your brain
it's far beyond the madness
buried deep beneath your fear
under all the doubt and worry
further still, you're near
once you're there
please be prepared
you won't want to come home
as you realise
heaven was inside you
hidden, all along.

A WRINKLE

What makes a wrinkle?
too much sun, too little sleep
lack of care for self?

I don't think so

in one wrinkle I can find
a hundred wholesome moments
where laughter flowed
full belly-sourced joy
till cheeks ached in happy

in one wrinkle I can find
a million smiles, sunrises
the infectious delight of a baby's giggle

in one wrinkle I can find
a myriad troubles and hard times
which took away peace
but were overcome
leaving us stronger
more *ourselves*

in one wrinkle I can find
so much proof of life
and yes
perhaps too many days
spent in the sun
lucky us.

"

Put your hand on your chest
and feel that heartbeat pulsing
through your body

"

WHAT IF?

What if you're never ready? What if, this is as close to
being ready that you'll ever actually be? What if, the
biggest regret you have when you look back on your life
is that you wasted time waiting to be better, when you
were already enough? What if, the last thought you have
when your life comes to an end, is that you didn't do
enough living whilst you could? My friend, this is it.
This is your life, right here, right now. Somebody
somewhere went to sleep last night assuming tomorrow
would be a new day. And it wasn't. Today is the day.
Every day is the day. Life waits for no one. Seize the
moment, seize the day. Dance. Watch the sunset. Eat the
cake. Put your bare feet on the cool grass. Be alive. Put
your hand on your chest and feel that heartbeat pulsing
through your body. That's all you need to be ready.
That is truly all the purpose you ever really need. You,
my friend, are alive. So *live*.

MAY

May your days be filled with laughter
may your chores complete themselves
may your mind have time to wander
to a sandy beach of shells

may your morning stretch be graceful
may your lunch be full of taste
may your inspiration find you
may no moment go to waste

may your lonely days be lacking
may your friendships linger strong
may your thoughts be full of wonder
may your worries all be gone

may your money flow like water
may your problems float away
may your needs be met and more so
may you wake to sunny days

may you find the strength inside you
may you learn to look within
may you see yourself more kindly
may that journey now begin.

NOW THAT I AM OLDER

The list of things I want
has grown smaller
with every passing year
these days
I can pretty much narrow it down to
good health for us all
enough money, enough time
enough fun, enough adventure
enough work
really, just enough

the list of things I don't want, however
has grown bigger, a whole lot bigger

at the top of that list
comes unnecessary drama

as I get older I realise
that I can handle pretty much
any negativity or adversity
life may throw my way
but I don't have to
I don't have to sign up for it all
it's pretty freeing
in fact, I can cancel my subscription
to anyone's drama, anytime I please
and I have
if it costs you your peace
it's too expensive, right?
spend wisely, my friend
this life is yours.

66

May you always understand you are
complete, may you never feel
the need to compete

99

DAUGHTER

I hope you know you are made from the very best
of me. Like a glittering disco ball, created from only
the finest of my shards, you were created to shine ever
bright. To reflect, absorb and radiate pure light. Love
was the glue and the final parts of you, were carved by
your own hand. May you always understand, you are
complete. May you never feel the need to compete. And
when you run low, when you don't know where to go,
remember our love knows no bounds. It grows fierce in
the deepest of grounds. Daughter, you are never alone.
In your heart lives your home. Made from all that
boundless love, from which you were grown.

A WOMAN WITHOUT HER MOTHER

If you are a woman
without her mother
there will never be a day
you don't miss her

never a day, where you don't wish
you could hear her voice
or ask for her advice just one more time

there will never be a moment
that you don't regret a missed visit
simply because life was too busy
and now you realise busy is fake, it isn't real
she was real and she is gone
and you are without her

the feeling of abandonment
and loneliness is mind-blowing
no matter how loved
or surrounded by family you may be
none of it is her

when the woman who
brought you into this world
or raised you up
is no longer here
it is a lonely place

and you are now she
you are now the one expected to guide
to discipline, to love
to handle everything for everyone
and that is a shock

but, truly, you've got this
because she taught you well

she made you right
and she made you strong
filled you with enough love
to last when she was gone

so, go on
and make her proud

and remember
look out for the little girl
who still lives inside you somewhere

she misses her mama very much

be kind.

TAKE ALL I HAVE

They say kindness is the giving
I believe that to be true
so many gifts I passed along
that blossomed where they flew

and of the things I have in life
none truly are my own
this universe is linked by love
and people are our homes

when I'm gone take all I have
and scatter it for miles
and plant within the soil of soul
the imprint of my smile

when I am light and love so free
give everything away
my body must be shared
to see another live their days

my soul was always more than me
so all of me is yours
when I am light and love so free
my kindness will endure.

*A poem for organ donation awareness

NEITHER MERRY NOR BRIGHT

If you haven't sent cards this year, or you've forgotten
someone's gift. If you don't have matching pyjamas or
a festive family photograph. It's okay. If you can't find
the energy to be merry and bright, or your tree isn't even
decorated yet, that's *fine*. If you don't feel like watching
your favourite Christmas movies, or honouring the
traditions that you normally always do. Don't sweat it,
my friend. These things don't matter. This year has been
hard. Really hard. If you can't see a way to celebrating
like you have in the past, don't worry. Just hang on in
there, letting in any joy you can, in any little way. Just
make it through till next year, for a new view. One day at
a time. We need you. Hang on in there. You are loved.

THE BATTLE OF YOUR BODY

You weren't supposed to battle
with your body
your body was never supposed
to be your fight

life was supposed to be the fight
survival was supposed to be the challenge
and peace was supposed to be the aim

your body was gifted
to get you through
the other wars you face

it's a body of great design
and amazing resilience

you are the top of the body tree
in Mother Nature's kingdom

your body was never supposed to be
your battle, my friend
it was supposed to be the ship
that sailed you to new shores
to taste life in all its glory
and adventure
the way humans were made to

your body is the house to host your soul
and attract all the other like-minded souls
into your garden

if you're trapped battling your body
it's time to stop

when illness comes
your body needs you
as a friend
as a teammate

to battle the attackers
not to *be* one

listen to your body
it knows nothing of the current fashion
or the way people look around you
it's doing its job
and it needs what it needs

give it what it needs

but above all give it acceptance

you don't have to love it
but you do have to accept it
otherwise, peace will never be achieved
in your time on this earth

wouldn't that be a sad thing indeed.

Maybe you're not
breaking apart
maybe you're
breaking open

MAKING DO

I wondered
where all the good things were

I thought maybe
they were passing me by
despite my constant searching of the sky
for their arrival, so
I just busied myself with survival

and year by year I waited for them to land
like glittering jewels in my upturned hands

until eventually hopes began to wane
perhaps I had misread the rules of this game

it was then I realised
as sparkling rays cut through cloudy skies
that the good things in my life had already arrived
right in front of my eyes

they were the things with which
I was *making do*

the messy, imperfect loves
and the ugly, hard-to-share truths

they were me
and they were you

fields of gold and waters blue.

"

Breathe into self-acceptance
and fight the inner critic
who shames you

"

UNIVERSE IN SKIN

Why don't we practise only noticing things about
each other that have nothing to do with our shape?
When you're on the beach, say. Breathe into self-
acceptance and fight the inner critic who shames you, but
don't let her pick at others either. Take each thought
and flip it. Look at that older woman being totally
present and free with her grandkids. Look at that young
woman clearly feeling the wind in her hair. And whilst
we are doing this, let's stop clicking on articles about
women's bodies and how they have changed. Let's take a
stand, come together and protect one another from this
cage of conformity. Your shape is the least interesting
thing about you, about any of us, and focusing so hard
on it has distracted us from seeing the full wonder within
our unique selves. Each of us is a universe in skin. And
the skin is the least important part.

TO THE TEACHERS

Thank you to the teachers
who work harder than we see
always finding ways
to weave turmoil into glee

thank you to the teachers
who see faces in their heads
as they try to close their eyes
and put their busy brains to bed

thank you to the teachers
who hold all those faces dear
little faces full of worry
small faces full of fear

thank you to the teachers
who note what others don't
the reason for the shyness
and the sad behind the *won't*

thank you to the teachers
who race the clock each day
finding balance between time
and the urge to stop and play

thank you to the teachers
we are grateful for this start
please know, you've a forever home
in so many children's hearts.

SPINSTER

Spinster: an old woman left on the shelf. Bitter, lonely and stiff. Or so we were led to believe, to fear this fate befalling us. But now we know ... spinster actually meant a woman who weaved and spun so well she was financially independent. She did not need to be owned by a man. She could remain as she was, if she wished. Not dismissed, not undesired, just able to live, earn, weave and pay her own way. Spinster, they called us. And we heard *unwanted*. When we should have heard ... *free*.

A MOTHER'S HEART

It is hard to watch your hatchlings fly, I know

but you're a seasoned pro
at letting go

you let go
the precious newborn
who held your heart in tiny fist

and then your cherub toddler left
and so begins the list

the four-year-old
with widened eyes
who questioned every thing

the five-year-old
so full of life
who taught your soul to sing

the eight-year-old
whose bravery daily
took your breath away

the nine-year-old
who'd run through darkness
safe, to where you lay

the ten-year-old
with silent fears
that shook your battered heart

the twelve-year-old
who braced themselves
for teenagehood to start

you loved them all
with every step

and let them all depart

the wonders of this world

cannot explain a mother's heart.

WEAR THE BREEZE

Yes, encouraging one another *to wear the shorts*,
is a body-positive siren call. But have you ever thrown
on a cool, flowing kaftan? Or a soft floaty dress with
no buttons and zips to pinch or restrict, and felt
anything but wonderful? There are so many ways
to liberate our bodies. And everyone is different.
But perhaps showing skin is not actually a measure
of how at peace you are within your home. Maybe,
the only measure of that, is lack of care for what
others think of your attire at all. I'm just saying, in
case it hadn't yet crossed your mind, that an army of
goddess women in free-flowing, colourful kaftans
and soft, serving garments – letting the breeze in
and keeping the judgement out – sounds pretty
liberating to me.

THE CHANGE

The change, they call it
but don't teach you how
to sleep through the night
with a sweat-laden brow

to manage the days
with a brain full of fog
to navigate life
when each task is a slog

we're not taught to cope
with the ups and the downs
the hormones that ride
on a merry-go-round

the itch and prickle
the dryness of skin
the strange sensory world
that we find ourselves in

yet as women we know
that to live is to change
so, we learn to adapt
and evolve once again

we gather together
to share hidden truths
together we wave
at the ghosts of our youth

like the phoenix we rise
from the ash and the rubble
made stronger again
no strangers to trouble

a sisterhood bonded
by spiritual thread
we won't be held down
till the day we are dead.

SKIN TIGHT

Maybe my skin was just too tight
that's why I never felt comfortable in it

I know if my jeans are too tight
I'm miserable all day
smothered, bothered, uneasy

but now, now my skin is loose
it feels right somehow

like a favourite sweater that hugs
silently radiating support
but never rubbing or pinching

perhaps that was the issue all along

I was just waiting on my skin
letting go a little

so I could do the same.

"

With arms soft as air
a laugh full of rainbows
and clouds for hair

"

GRANNY

A place to go when no other fits, there's no
comfort quite like a granny, who *sits*. And *listens,*
with earnest, unwavering care. A granny has time, like
she's going nowhere. She's right here, in the moment,
with arms soft as air and a laugh full of rainbows
and clouds for hair. She knows when you're sad, you
can tell her your dreams, each word that you speak is
important, you're *seen*. A place to rest when the world
is too much and noises, too loud, a granny is such a
gift. When she's near, you're never alone. My Gran,
dear Granny, you feel just like home.

THE UGLY DAYS

On the ugly days
when you wake
with that feeling of self-disgust
we all have them
when your skin feels like someone else's
and your face holds no sparkle or life

do not look in the mirror
to find yourself again

look at the memories
the moments that live in your mind
the days when you shone

look at the times
you made someone else
feel beautiful again, or loved

look at the way
your body wakes every day
and moves you around in this world
to spread kindness and be *you*

look at the features
passed down to you
by those you loved so very much
and those they loved too

on the ugly days
you won't find your worth in the mirror
but you will find it in the memories.

FLOWING WITH

It doesn't matter if you're 20, 50 or 80, in this life,
you will feel like a child sometimes. You will feel like
you've learned nothing in your time here on earth, like
you're starting again from scratch. You will feel hopeless
sometimes too, abandoned, rejected. It doesn't matter
how much money you have or how sharp your learned
wisdom may be, life will strip you naked now and again,
to show you who is boss. Spoiler alert: it's not you. Life
flows from its own mysterious source, and we have two
choices: to flow *with* or *against*. My money is on *with*.
And if you're flowing with, you must be ready to feel it
all. Have a scream, curl up tight and let the river
wash you to a new dawn.

Don't live life
against the wind
let go, see where
you fly

HAVE THE COURAGE

Have the courage
to live as a whole
to listen to your heart
to talk to your soul

to know who you are
when others do not
to look out for vibes
to filter your thoughts

have the heart
to shoulder the world
to see that we're one
whether woman or girl

to understand life
is a pathway of love
that the kingdom of heaven
is right here, not above

have the joy
to appreciate life
to laugh and to cry
to accept both are right

to go with the flow
when the winds of change rage
to learn to let go
to break free from that cage

have the vision
to share your own story
the ugly truth heals
as much as the glory

pass down your lessons
the joy and the pain
remind those who follow
growth happens in rain

have the patience
to search for the signs
but never stop living
enjoying the ride

listen to silence
as loud as the screams
respect life's sorrows
make space for your dreams.

BEING A MOTHER

Being a mother is wearing your heart
outside of your body
for the rest of your life, maybe more
it's joy and worry and heartache and fear
all mixed in
like a wonderful kaleidoscope of love
so many colours

being a mother is bearing the weight
of a thousand rocks
on your shoulders, every day
yet we would bear those rocks
and more, gladly, given the choice
again and again

being a mother is laughter and noise
and messy kisses
it's soft hugs and salty tears
to wipe away

motherhood is a joy
like you've never known before
with pain and confusion
am I enough?

not being a mother
is the hardest journey
for some women to take
they would walk on glass, for eternity
to hold that little soul in their arms
such grief, such loss

having a mother is a blessing
not bestowed upon us all
she is your safe place, your anchor
your home

when she is gone, the world is amiss
and you'd give
anything you have and more
for one more hug

for the mothers, the daughters, the aunties
the carers, the foster parents
the teachers, and anyone
who takes a child into their hearts
you are blessed
you are loved
and you should be celebrated

every day.

66

As one, we are almost opposite
day and night, full moon and
bright sunlight

99

SISTER

Sometimes I think my sister and I are the same person broken apart, like those necklace charms you can piece together to make a heart. As one, we are almost opposite: day and night, full moon and bright sunlight. But together we create a unique energy … as though we were always meant to be. Created to exist at the same time. And somehow, in the hardest of climbs, our power arrives. Together, our strength seems to multiply. As though magic is made when we connect to each other, a force that could not be, without one another. Sisters, half moon, half sun.

Apart we exist, together we *become*.

THINGS I WOULD TELL MY YOUNGER SELF

You don't need to wait
for the right person to come into your life
you can become the right person in your life
everyone else will be the icing on your cake

success can be measured by
how peaceful the sleep
not how busy the day

if being more *you*
pushes people away
they were never supposed to be there

feelings are visitors, all of them
allow them to pass through with grace
but open the window
when it's time for them to leave

don't attach your self-worth
to something that moves
you are so much more than your looks
your possessions, or your relationships

hardening up for this hardened world
will only make this hardened world harder

staying soft is where the true strength lies
and anyway, your warmth will melt
some of the hardness you come up against

be wary of fitting in, it often requires you
to cut out pieces of your starlit soul
that might just be your very best parts

approval, real approval
can only come from one source, *yourself*
everything else is opinion

being different isn't easy
but being fake is much harder
and will eat you from the inside out

stop every now and again
to look back
see how far you have come

and whilst you are there, gaze up
at the dazzling, bejewelled night sky
imagine every star is a person
you have made smile along the way

there is magic and beauty
in every single thing
if you learn how to look for it

life is hard, it hurts
but the beauty of it heals, too
do not pick at the wounds as they do

life is short but feels long
if you are travelling in disguise
loaded down with shame

travel light, love weighs nothing
acceptance is your constant companion
and hope is your GPS

eyes wide, heart open
really feel, really *see*
what an adventure you embark upon

each day your eyes flutter awake
to behold another sunrise
no matter how clouded the light

is a gift that only you can open

what a thing.

"

There is magic and beauty
in every single thing
if you learn how to look for it

"

MY MOTHER'S HANDS

When my face does not fit, I look
for my granny's nose
for my father's chin
for the strong signs of those before me
and before them

I search inside my bones for those I love
and I hold my mother's hands
in front of my face in prayer
when my body feels alien
I remember where it came from, who it carried
who it carries *still*
when my skin is a prison
I go into my DNA and gaze in wonder
at the events which compounded
to create my life

when my face does not fit
I find their faces
and it brings me home.

YOUR TIME

The only order that truly exists, is the natural order.
Birth, childhood, puberty, adulthood, old age. The rest
is man-made. And I don't care for man-made, when
it comes to my life and its timeline. You decide when
you are ready to choose your career, maybe you'll even
have a handful. Perhaps none of those callings will
have anything in common at all, except you. You, and
only you, will know when and if marriage is right.
When and if your body clock ticks to procreate. When
and if your marriage is no longer right or your life
is in need of a drastic re-form. If you do one thing
whilst you are here, run to your natural clock, and not
society's. Only one tells *your* time.

THE SEASON OF LETTING GO

And so begins the season of letting go
when Mother Nature shows us all
how it's done
let go
free yourself
shake it off
drop it
give way for the new
create space for new thoughts, new ideas
new adventures and new connections
by shedding the dead weight
you've been carrying around
for so long
and whilst you are there
being reborn and renewed
let go of old anxieties too
let go of any doubts, fears or beliefs
which no longer serve you well
release bitterness or past hurts
which feast on your beauty
be brave
don't fear the nakedness
as your leaves slip away
Mother Nature doesn't

watch and learn.

YOUR BODY

Your body does not belong to them
the *industries*

those who sell you
last-minute diets
then watch in glee
as you lose yourself
amongst the treats
before calling you back
as you descend
into a spiral of guilt
to begin another year
or summer

they want you
exhausted
they want you
ashamed
they want you
desperate
to spend your hard-earned money

but your body does not need them
my friend
your body
in fact
knows exactly what it needs

it needs rest
it needs light
fresh air
it needs water
acceptance
kindness
it even needs fun

most of all
it needs not to be bombarded

with everything at once
and then nothing at all

enjoy your meals
eat with peace
with love
never **guilt**
guilt festers and rots

your body is not a display piece
for the world to judge

it is your home
it is where you do your *living*

and a little bit of cheer
need never deplete you
of your *peace*.

THAT'S HOW STORIES WORK

You can't delete chapters in your own story
that's not how stories work
you have to face each page, each twist, each turn
you have to live out each and every chapter
from the start to the end
some of those chapters won't be pretty
we each get our share
of good and bad in this life
though it may often seem unfairly split
it's really not
we all go through ups, we all go through downs
some days we laugh
and other days
we can barely breathe for crying
there are times
when the crying feels like it will never stop
but it will
and a new chapter will begin when it does
but with each chapter comes a very important step
in your journey
and we can't rewrite them, because if we did
we wouldn't be who we are now
and the world needs you just the way you are
broken, beautiful
and a better person for it too
you can't remove chapters in your own story
and if you care, or dare, to share your tales
(the good and the ugly)
you may be just the inspiration someone else desperately
needs, so, pass it down
that's how stories work.

"

If friends grew in nature
you would no doubt be a sunflower

"

FRIEND

What a gift it is in this life to have a friend. The kind
on which you can always depend. A friend like you.
Who seems to arrive with the glue, right on time. The
perfect partner in crime. And if friends grew in nature,
you would no doubt be a sunflower. So bright, so full
of sunshine-seeking power, storing light for darkest
hours. Petals facing the sun. Heart open, ready to run.
Always finding the fun. My friend. You have been the
laughter when life was empty. You have given me back
permission to *be*. Helped me find the woman I had
forgotten to see. I hope I do that for you. I hope I'm
always your glue. Here's to me loving you. My friend.
Today. Tomorrow. Until the end.

The perfect body
like the perfect day
is something only
you can call

YOU WEREN'T BORN TO FADE AWAY

Life may smooth away all of your rough edges
with its twists and turns and lessons to be learned
life may force you to fashion a tough outer shell
life may break you and reform you many, many times
until you don't even recognise the shapes
you see in the mirror anymore
and that's okay, it really is
just don't let life make you smaller
don't let anyone convince you that your cracks
your scars, are a sign of weakness
they are war wounds, my friend
battles fought and survived
they are your story, your fight, your journey
let life reshape you over and over again, sure
but don't let it make you fade away
fading away is not what you are here for
let peace fill your heart as the years go by
and your wisdom abounds
let anger and pettiness fall from its pedestal
but don't let your voice diminish
there are countless young women out there
who need to hear you and hear you loudly
you weren't put on this earth
to burn brightly
then fade away
get louder
you have much more to say now.

AGE-OLD SCARS

I'm working on a range of compliments that don't
trigger age-old scars, made by the tearing of our
self-worth, too soon. Compliments that don't hint
at a before or after, a better or worse, a time when
you were more or less. Compliments that deliver the
message firmly to the soul, without hint of surface-
level conditions. Don't get me wrong, I'm never going
to stop telling you your look is fabulous, because it
is, and the way you create it, is like art, if you ask
me. But, I won't tell you you look in great shape, or
young for your age. I will never help you cling to your
youthful self when the woman you are becoming
every day is a sight for sore eyes and souls. And nor
will I believe, for a minute, that less of your flesh is
something worth celebrating, more than the effect
your presence has on my levels of joy, safety and
friendship. I'm working on a range of compliments
that banish the stock phrases we know so well.
I think: it is definitely time.

A SMALL VOICE

I heard a small voice
in the darkness one day
she whispered, sweet child
it's your moment to stray

it's high beyond time
that you saw who you are
a soul wearing atoms
once housed in a star

let go of the bars
that have held you so long
and clear some things out
whilst your fortitude's strong

the dysfunctional relationships
the caring too much
the living a life
so far out of touch

come back to the source
come back to the calm
break out of the *cool*
come lie where it's *warm*

the giving too much
the beating of self
the worry you'll rot
on an imaginary shelf

come back where the fear
is a friend not a foe
remember the thrill
of release, let it go

run like a child
as the school doors spring free
sing like a bird
in the strongest of trees

live like a woman
who's been to the core
the gift is the freedom
and there's always
much more.

"

You didn't lose anything
you gifted it

"

YOUR PINK

They say flamingos lose their pink when they give birth, but you didn't lose your pink, dear mamas. You *gave* it, ounce by ounce, to your greatest ever love. You sacrificed every little bit of your goodness, of your colour, so they could grow more colourful still. You didn't lose anything. You gifted it. And in time, you will grow yourself some more. Cell by cell, you will create that colour, just like you created the wonder of star, universe and soul that is your baby. Because creating is what you do. And the simple act of knowing this … *knowing* that their pink, their outrageously glorious pink, was once yours, will make your new pink grow much faster. And in fact, you may not even choose pink this time. Maybe you'll choose yellow. Why not? You're not the same, after all. How could you be? You imploded to make another human. Like the universe did to make you. What art. What magic. What *colour*.

A BIG FAN OF WOMEN

I'm a big fan of women with raucous laughs
women who overshare awkward truths
when the conversation stalls

I'm a lover of singing loudly in the car
and I love pulling alongside a fellow diva
doing the same

I'm a big fan of women who love women
who spot lipstick on teeth
and help each other out
when Mother Nature calls

I'm a huge believer in comparison
being the thief of joy
that dimming someone else's light
won't ever make yours shine more brightly

I just can't get enough of those women
who are unashamedly themselves
in technicolour glory

I'm a lover of laughter and those moments
when the tears of joy start to flow, give me life

I think the best therapy is quality time with a friend
who listens without judgement
I'm a big fan of women who break, who share
who rebuild each other and cheer along the way
I'm grateful for this world half-full of fabulous females
I see you all, each and every one.

REMAIN WHOLE

I hope you can remain whole, for that quest to be
your goal. Not to let loss take parts of you away.
The best parts of those you miss, can stay. You can
decide to *be* those things, let their love provide you with
wings. And when you fall in love anew. It is not required
for you, to lay parts of yourself to rest. To continue
with *less*. Love is never a test. It should always feel like
more. Never fear that you have no space to store ... the
heart can expand. It can outgrow the universe and all
the land. You will break. Make no mistake. And your
parts will be glued back in different shapes. You'll be
rearranged, new versions of you will feel strange,
but you will be whole. And I hope you will see, that
was always the goal.

GRACE TO SLOW

Pray, grant me the space to grow
bless me with the grace to *slow*

when all around is fire and rising
let me cast my old disguise in

help me know, when it's time to lay low
to become flow, to let control go

when tempers flare and panic sets
let me cast my safety net, of faith
let me be my *own* safe

pray, grant me the space to grow
and the unending desire to sow
seeds of peace

let my need to win release
let me honour loud my grief
keep my heart on deep belief

grant me space to grow, *pray*
give me grace to slow.

"

No woman left behind
no woman left behind

"

WHEN ONE WOMAN SCREAMS

When one woman screams, I think all women hear.
All women feel that scream as it twists their gut.
Somehow. And when those women are silenced, in fear,
in hiding, in hell, when that one woman cannot scream
any longer, we all must scream for her. And we do.
When the world turns and some women are forced to go
back instead of forward, we don't imagine for a moment
that this is not our issue. No woman left behind. *No
woman left behind*. When one woman screams, all
women listen. I hear it. I know you do too.

CHANGE THE WAY YOU SEE

I don't have crow's feet
I have happy, happy memories
of laughing with friends until the tears flowed

I don't have frown lines
I have the marks of my frustration and confusion
which I battled through, smiling in the end

I am not going grey
I have shimmering highlights of wisdom
dashed throughout my silver hair

I don't have scars
I have symbols of the strength I was able to find
when life got tough

I don't have stretch marks
I have the marks of growth
and the marks of motherhood
my womanly evolution

I am not fat
I bear the evidence of a life
filled with abundance
with blessings and good times

I am not just forgetful
I have a mind so full of stories
memories and moments
there is scarce room to hold much else

I am not old
I am blessed, with a life of great length
something not everyone can say

don't change the way you look
my friend
change the way you see

change the way
you see.

"

We are free, and we are more
powerful than ever

"

WOMEN, NOT WITCHES

Make no mistake, it was women like you, like me, who
burned on those pyres for their *witchcraft*. Women
who listened to their instincts, who connected with
other souls on unseen levels. Women who healed, who
loved bravely and who saw what some eyes couldn't.
Women who shone too brightly for those in fear of their
powers. You, my friend, should carry that light even
more fiercely now, in honour of those who were put out
in flame. We are free, we are more powerful than ever.
And anyone who fears that will show their true colours
in the dazzling light of our own. Yes, we carry that
witch wound with us. But we glow harder for it.

A WOMAN'S WOMAN

She's a woman's woman
she's been through enough
to recognise your mask
to remember what it feels like
what she needed, when *she* was *you*
so she gives it freely without question

she's a keeper of secrets
a gentle teller of hard truths
a listener
she's a healer of pain
a foul-weather friend

she shows up for the dark times
because she knows that when it's light
you don't need her quite the same

she's a woman's woman
and she knows
what it takes to be you, every day
to be all things to so many

she knows how much this life
can drain the soul
and she is there to fill that up again

she's a woman's woman
and you have been blessed.

HOW YOU ARE

When I ask you this question, I want to know, if light
is winning over your dark today. If joy is succeeding
in her quest to enter erratically, at will. I am asking if
your worth is intact, or if it has absconded once more,
attached to something it should never have touched, like
the nonsensical lure of a hot plate. I am asking if sad
has visited you recently and if you let her in this time, to
chat it all out. And as you tell me your tales of how you
overslept again, the work you missed to clear your head
and the argument in which you found yourself losing
your cool, I hear: light winning over dark, joy cracking
flagstones for the briefest of beats and a worth that is
slowly growing back. When I ask how you are, I mean,
tell me what hurts. I'm listening. *I'm listening.*

66

All this time you've been shining
your light of refuge

99

LIGHTHOUSING

All this time, you've been *lighthousing*
quite unaware
of your brilliance

all this time
you've been shining your light of refuge
so brightly
in the darkest of seas
so those in peril will find a new route
around the ragged rocks

all this time
you've been saving lives
with your unending capacity
for rescuing souls in need
with your shine

a lighthouse

all this time

and you didn't even know it.

"

You are loud, you are passionate
you are messy, and that's a beautiful
thing to behold

"

TAKE UP SPACE

The best advice I could give any young woman is not to wish yourself smaller. You must take up space in this world – how else will you make the impact you were born to? Don't wish yourself less, either: you are loud, you are passionate, you are messy, and that's a beautiful thing to behold. The world needs you to be big. The world needs you to be bold. The world cries for you to break and rebuild without shame and stop apologising for everything you're not. You must take up space in this world. Don't *shrink*. Never *shrink*.

AFTERWORD

I hope you will turn to this book and open randomly, whenever you need to be reminded that you are not alone, *never* alone. The thread that connects us women is ancient, mystical and stretches farther than we know. Even the silent screams can be heard, deep within our gut. When you need your sisters, let the universe know. We will come. We will come.

ACKNOWLEDGEMENTS

As always, my acknowledgements begin at the feet of the women who brought this to life. A book may only have impact if it is read, and shared. Thank you to each and every one of you who became part of this happening. The women who wove these words into their friendship groups and families. And thank you to those who have remained with me all the way, through so many more books, lessons and new versions of ourselves.

To those just finding me, a thank you to you too. You are so welcome and so needed.

Thank you also to the women in the core of my life. My mum, whom my dad has always referred to as the original witch, and my sister, the elder witch-in-training. I make three and we are so lucky to be so close in heart, and geographically now too. I never take a moment for granted.

Thank you to my beautiful friends, without whom life would be colourless and unsafe. And thank you to my editor Susanna, whom I now count as a friend too.

Thank you to my team at Bonnier for giving this book her moment in the sun she so deserves. What a joy it is to see her cloaked in finery after her humble beginnings.

ABOUT THE AUTHOR

Donna Ashworth is a *Sunday Times* bestselling poet who lives in the hills of Scotland with her husband, two sons, Brian and Dave (the dogs), and Sheldon (the cat). Donna started her social media accounts in 2018 in a bid to create a 'safe' social space for women to come together and connect, but her love of all things wordy quickly became the focus and a past love for poetry was reignited. Over ten books and 1.8 million followers later, Donna is delighted daily with her mission to shower the world with words and make poetry a go-to in our wellbeing toolkit.

'I believe wholeheartedly in the power of opening a daily poetry page to better everyone's mental health and clear space within our minds. Poetry is permission to feel everything we as humans are absolutely supposed to, knowing we are not alone, never alone. Poetry is not folly for the fancy; it is using words to shift perspectives, heal wounds and let in light again. And it is something we can pass to one another when times become turbulent, as they so often will. Open this book at random, whenever you need a message or a focus or a sign … the book just knows. As do you, my friends, as do you.'

Facebook @DonnaAshworth
Instagram @DonnaAshworthWords
TikTok @DonnaAshworthWordy
X @donna_ashworth

IF YOU ENJOYED THIS COLLECTION, YOU MAY ALSO ENJOY:

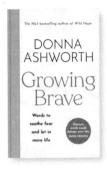

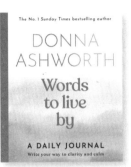

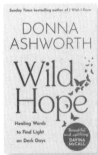

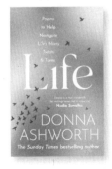

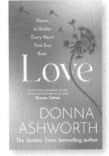

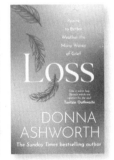